These Are My Friends on
Politics

Written and Illustrated by Billy O'Keefe

INKSHARES

Published by Inkshares, Inc., San Francisco, California
www.inkshares.com

Edited and designed by Girl Friday Productions
www.girlfridayproductions.com
Cover design by Billy O'Keefe and Paul Barrett
Illustrations by Billy O'Keefe

ISBN: 9781942645238
e-ISBN: 9781942645245
Library of Congress Control Number: 2016938875

10 9 8 7 6 5 4 3 2 1

First edition October 2016. Printed by RR Donnelley.

Printed in China

To Mom, Dad, Chrystal, and everyone out there who drew a little heart-shaped circle around the second Wednesday in November on their calendars

HI. THIS IS ME. BUT ENOUGH ABOUT ME. THIS ISN'T MY STORY.

NOPE, IT'S ABOUT THEM.
THESE ARE MY FRIENDS.

THEY'RE REGULAR FOLKS LIKE YOU AND ME. THEY HAVE HOPES, DREAMS, FEARS, RESPONSIBILITIES, HOBBIES, WEIRD SMARTPHONE BRAND LOYALTIES, TEN THOUSAND UNREAD EMAILS, NO TIME IN THE DAY TO MARK THOSE EMAILS AS READ, AND NO INCLINATION TO JUST *SELECT THEM ALL* AND DELETE THEM *BECAUSE HEAVEN FORBID ONE OF THOSE EMAILS IS IMPORTANT.*

(PAGE THREE AND I'M ALREADY OFF TRACK. SORRY, MOVING ON.)

THESE ARE MY FRIENDS DOING NORMAL,
GROWN-UP THINGS, LIKE BEING LATE FOR WORK
AND PAYING THEIR BILLS (MOSTLY) ON TIME.

THESE ARE MY FRIENDS DOING FUN THINGS FRIENDS DO, LIKE LAUGHING AND ENJOYING A MEAL TOGETHER.

AND THESE ARE MY FRIENDS ON POLITICS.
THE END. THANKS FOR READING.

JUST KIDDING.
LET'S BACK UP.
SO WHAT HAPPENED HERE?

IT STARTS INNOCENTLY ENOUGH,
USUALLY WITH A STORY IN THE NEWS.

AFTER EVERYONE ENTHUSIASTICALLY
AFFIRMS THAT THEY ARE TOTALLY FAMILIAR
WITH THIS NEWS STORY,[1] A DISCUSSION ENSUES.

1. Just the headline, I should clarify. No one here actually bothered to read the story.[2]

2. Though two of them have commented on and/or shared it anyway.

AND AFTER AN EARNEST FIVE-MINUTE[1] ATTEMPT TO DISCUSS THE STORY OBJECTIVELY, SOMEONE FINALLY[2] CAVES AND CASUALLY CLAIMS THE WHOLE THING IS PARTY #1'S FAULT...

1. Actually four minutes and thirty-one seconds, but the mood is still upbeat at this point, so I'm generously rounding up.

2. Yes, the "finally" is sarcasm. Mood is souring quickly. Hold on tight.

... AFTER WHICH POINT SOMEONE ELSE CLEVERLY RETORTS THAT, FOR TOTALLY OPPOSITE YET SOMEHOW IDENTICAL REASONS, IT'S ALL PARTY #2'S FAULT ...

...BUT NEVER THE FAULT OF BOTH PARTIES OR THEIR INABILITY TO CO OP ER AT E OR THE OBVIOUS FACT THAT SOME THINGS ARE TOO BIG FOR POLITICS ALONE TO JUST MAGICALLY FIX—

OH, SORRY. MOVING ON.

SOMEONE THEN WILL POINT OUT THAT THE ONE PARTY'S CANDIDATE / MOST PROMINENT ELECTED OFFICIAL[1] SAID A DUMB THING ABOUT WHATEVER HAPPENED . . .

1. Circle one depending on whether it's election season or not.[2] 2. Just kidding, it's always election season these days. Circle both.

. . . WHICH SOMEONE ELSE WILL COUNTER BY SLAMMING THE OTHER CANDIDATE, WHO SAID BASICALLY THE SAME ABSURD THING IN A DIFFERENT AND SOMEHOW WORSE WAY.[1]

1. Don't worry, fans of this candidate! Candidate #1, predictably, counters with something even more preposterously clueless.[2]

2. Which, unfortunately, Candidate #2 outdoes not even twenty-four hours later. Sorry.[3] 3. But don't worry! Because—

UPON DISCOVERY THAT IT IS MORE INSTANTLY GRATIFYING TO INSULT THESE POLITICIANS[1] THAN IT IS TO EXPLORE THE ISSUE,[2] OTHER ISSUES INEXPLICABLY SLIDE INTO THE MIX.[3]

1. Scientifically speaking, "your party stinks" functions here as the control variable. 2. These issues constitute the independent variable. 3. This creates the out-of-control variable. (Get it? Because of all the yelling that follows!)

THESE, FOR INSTANCE, ARE MY FRIENDS
ON HEALTH CARE (AND/OR THE EVILS AND/OR
VIRTUES OF SOCIALISM AND/OR CAPITALISM)[1] . . .

1. Current "If X happens, I'll just move to Canada" count: Two.

. . . AND EDUCATION . . .

(I *THINK* WE'RE ALL IN FAVOR OF EDUCATION, BUT AT
THIS STAGE IT SOMETIMES GETS DIFFICULT TO TELL.)

... THE TWO AMENDMENTS OF THE UNITED STATES CONSTITUTION THAT EVERYONE HAS HEARD OF (YOU KNOW, THE FIRST TWO)...

(IT JUST HIT YOU RIGHT NOW THAT YOU HAVE *NO IDEA* WHAT THE THIRD AMENDMENT IS ABOUT, DIDN'T IT? ADMIT IT, IT DID.)

. . . AND THE WAR . . .

. . . THE OTHER WAR . . .

... THE WAR WE SHOULD OR SHOULD NOT START
AFTER WE'RE I GUESS DONE WITH THESE OTHER WARS ...

... AND THE VARIOUS WARS ON WOMEN, MEN, MINORITIES, MAJORITIES, THE PLANET, SMALL BUSINESSES, CORPORATIONS, UNIONS, WALL STREET, MAIN STREET, DRUGS, LEGALIZATION OF DRUGS, SUGAR, GLUTEN, THE POOR, THE RICH, THE MIDDLE-CLASS, FARMERS, BANKERS, MARRIAGE, SINGLE MOMS, SINGLE DADS, PRIVACY, VALUES, CHILDREN, SENIORS, KETCHUP ON HOTDOGS, THAT BILLY GOAT WHO CURSED THE CUBS, EVERYONE READING THIS BOOK, AND CHRISTMAS.

Check one: _ Making light of these issues = offensive. _ These "issues" = political correctness run amok. _ Humanity = doomed.

INVARIABLY AND INEVITABLY, THESE ARE
MY FRIENDS ON THE ECONOMY.

SPECIFICALLY, THE UNEMPLOYMENT RATE, WHICH EVERYONE CAN QUOTE TO A TENTH OF A PERCENT EVEN THOUGH EVERYONE'S NUMBER IS DIFFERENT AND EVERYONE AGREES THE NUMBER IS MEANINGLESS FOR DIFFERENT REASONS.

THEN THEY MOVE ON TO TAXES.

WHICH BASICALLY IS LIKE STARTING OVER AND GOING THROUGH EVERY ISSUE AGAIN EXCEPT WITH MONEY INVOLVED, WHICH OF COURSE ALWAYS GOES SUPER WELL.

THEN IT GETS RIDICULOUS.

(JUST KIDDING! IT'S BEEN RIDICULOUS
THIS WHOLE STUPID TIME.)

RIDICULOUS EXHIBIT A:

POLL NUMBERS "SCIENTIFICALLY GATHERED"
FROM A COLD-CALL PHONE SURVEY OF THIRTY PEOPLE
WHO WERE TOO POLITE TO JUST HANG UP THE PHONE.

RIDICULOUS EXHIBIT B:

STATISTICS THAT SAY ONE THING, THE OPPOSITE OF THAT THING, AND BASICALLY NOTHING OF ACTUAL VALUE ALL AT ONCE.

(THE PERSON WHO COINED THAT "NUMBERS DON'T LIE" PHRASE? TOTAL LIAR.)

RIDICULOUS EXHIBIT C: QUOTES CITING THE ANALYSIS[1] OF THOSE EXPERTS[2] ON THOSE TWENTY-FOUR-HOUR CABLE CHANNELS DEVOTED TO NEWS.[3]

1. Made-up, insane opinions, meant either to scare people or sell an equally insane book that was written to scare people. 2. Literally any other word but this one. Including some you aren't allowed to say on basic cable. 3. Screaming.

... AND RIDICULOUS EXHIBITS D THROUGH Z:

ABSOLUTELY INSANE STORIES
THAT COULD NOT POSSIBLY BE TRUE.

(A GOOD HALF OF WHICH I SWEAR I'VE READ IN THE *ONION*.)

HERE'S WHAT HAPPENS WHEN I SAY, "I'M PRETTY SURE THAT STORY IS FROM THE *ONION*!" OUTLOUD.

(EDITED FOR LANGUAGE OF COURSE. JUST IN CASE THERE ARE CHILDREN LOOKING OVER YOUR SHOULDER WHILE YOU'RE READING THIS.)[1]

1. Even though, make no mistake, every child older than nine knows all of these words. And probably a few you don't even know yet.

(IN CASE YOU WERE WONDERING IF ANYTHING HAS BEEN ACCOMPLISHED AT THIS POINT IN THE ARGUMENT, HERE'S A BONUS EXHIBIT THAT SUMS IT UP NICELY.)

Awesomeness Prime
@CWS102605 · 6m

Didn't know it was possible for all sides to lose a debate until tonight.
#YourWholePartyIsAJoke
#AttendedBetterPartiesAtWorkAndIHateMyJob

Respond · Rechirp · Like

Reply to @CWS102605

 @CWS102605 Wrong as usual #fakehashtagsarestupid #imdoingthisironicallytomakeapoint
2m

 @CWS102605 Terrible post, would not read again. Delete your account.
1m

 @CWS102605 Uhhh doesn't your boss follow you on here #oopsyoudiditagain
Just now

THANKS TO THE MAGIC OF TECHNOLOGY, THE ARGUMENT *NEVER* HAS TO END! HERE THEY ARE ON THAT ONE ANNOYING WEBSITE . . .

NameWitheld Hi NSA[1]

This whole debate has been embarressment! If any of these fools win,
I'm moving to Canada! Seriously! — feeling annoyed.

30 minutes • Public[2]

👍 5 people approve this message.

Approve Comment Share

 This thing needs a dislike button. So stupid!
29 minutes ago • Approve

 Speaking of "embarressment..."
20 minutes ago • Approve

 YOU'RE LUCKY CANADA'S CITIZENSHIP TEST DOESN'T HAVE A SPELLING AND GRAMMAR SECTION LOL
16 minutes ago • Approve

 adslk;;;
10 minutes ago • Approve • 👍 8

 ...
Just now • Approve

. . . AND, SIMULTANEOUSLY, THAT OTHER ANNOYING WEBSITE.

1 & 2. Painfully aware of this irony, yes.

AND BECAUSE NO ONE CAN LET ANYONE ELSE HAVE THE LAST WORD FOR EVEN A MOMENT, HERE THEY ARE TIDING THEMSELVES OVER ON APPS UNTIL THEY CAN USE THOSE WEBSITES TO TIDE THEMSELVES OVER UNTIL THEY CAN ANTAGONIZE EACH OTHER IN PERSON AGAIN.

SOMETIMES MY FRIENDS MEET UP IN PERSON
AND *STILL* INSULT EACH OTHER ON THESE WEBSITES
AND APPS WHILE I'M TRYING TO TELL WHAT *I*
THOUGHT WAS A PRETTY COOL STORY.

OK, CAN I JUST STOP AND
SAY SOMETHING HERE?

CAN WE DO SOMETHING ABOUT THIS NEED TO ENDLESSLY STARE AT OUR PHONES IN PUBLIC ALL THE TIME NOW? IS THE ACTUAL, LIVING WORLD[1] SO DULL THAT LOOKING AT A VIRTUAL, WATERED-DOWN VERSION OF IT[2] EVERY SIX MINUTES IS SOMEHOW MORE INTERESTING?

1. My pretty cool story! 2. Do you think I'd get a lot of likes if I posted this story on those websites?

DON'T TELL ANYONE I SAID THIS BECAUSE IT MAKES ME SOUND LIKE A MONSTER, BUT MY DREAM IS TO SEE, LIKE, EIGHT PEOPLE WHO ARE ALL MINDLESSLY STARING AT THEIR PHONES WHILE WALKING DOWN THE STREET, AND THEY ALL JUST CRASH INTO EACH OTHER AND DROP THEIR PHONES INTO NEARBY SEWER DRAINS. I THINK THAT WOULD BE *AWESOME.*

...WHOA. SORRY, OFF TRACK AGAIN. ANYWAY!

SO LOOK. I GET IT. IT'S NOT *ALL* POLITICS' FAULT. THE NEED TO BE RIGHT ABOUT EVERYTHING MEANS PEOPLE *ARGUE* ABOUT EVERYTHING. HERE ARE MY FRIENDS ARGUING ABOUT SPORTS . . .

... HERE THEY ARE ARGUING ABOUT A
MOVIE'S ENDING INSTEAD OF JUST, YOU
KNOW, LETTING IT PLAY OUT...

1. Nope. 2. Nope.

. . . HERE THEY ARE BLAMING OTHER CARS FOR BEING STUCK IN TRAFFIC, AS IF THE BOTTLENECK EFFECT IS SOMETHING ONLY PEOPLE WHO CAN'T DRIVE (ALSO KNOWN AS _____,[1] AM I RIGHT, FOLKS?!) CAN CAUSE . . .

1. Go ahead—write in the "liberal," "conservative," or whatever political affiliation you also use as a pejorative. Take your shot!

. . . AND HERE THEY ARE ARGUING ABOUT SOMETHING NONE OF THEM CAN EVEN REMEMBER.[1]

1. It was the economy again.[2]   2. Current "If X happens, I'll just move to Canada" count: 113.

I REALIZE WHAT YOU'RE ABOUT TO ASK
(OR PROBABLY ASKED AROUND PAGE TWENTY OR SO):
IF MY FRIENDS CANNOT EVEN CIVILLY DISCUSS
THIS STUFF, WHY EVEN BE FRIENDS AT ALL?

WELL, BECAUSE INEVITABLY, IN A FLASH OF CLARITY (AND/OR EXHAUSTION), EVERYONE RUNS OUT OF THINGS TO SAY, TIRES OF ARGUING ABOUT POLITICS, REALIZES HOW FRUITLESS THESE ARGUMENTS ARE, AND CALMS DOWN.

AND WE REALIZE THAT, EVEN THOUGH WE HAVE DIFFERENT IDEAS ABOUT HOW TO GET THERE, WE ALL BASICALLY WANT THE SAME THINGS FOR OURSELVES AND EACH OTHER, AND THEN WE'RE JUST FRIENDS AGAIN.[1]

1. FINAL SCORE: "He is inarguably the best president we've ever had": 63.
"He is inarguably the worst president we've ever had": 65. A real nail-biter!

AND, AS ~~TERRIFYING~~ PASSIONATE AS THEY
CAN BE, THESE *ARE MY* FRIENDS.

THESE ARE MY FRIENDS ON MY BIRTHDAY,
EVEN WHEN I DON'T REMIND THEM WHEN IT IS.

THESE ARE MY FRIENDS ON THE
DAY I GOT THE JOB I'D ALWAYS WANTED . . .

... AND ON THE DAY I GOT
LAID OFF SIX MONTHS LATER.[1]

1. Naturally, someone blamed the president specifically for this happening. Refer to the first
half of this book for an abstract illustration of what happened next. The "congratulations" banner
did not make it, but the piggy bank survived and is currently in hiding.

THESE ARE THE FRIENDS WHO ARE THERE
TO CELEBRATE THE BEST DAYS OF MY LIFE . . .

... AND CHEER ME UP ON THE WORST DAYS.

THESE ARE THE POLITICIANS MY FRIENDS AND I
CAN COUNT ON FOR THAT SAME KIND OF SUPPORT
ON THE BEST AND WORST DAYS OF OUR LIVES.
OR ANY DAY, FOR THAT MATTER.

(I'VE NEVER SEEN ONE. THAT'S THE JOKE.)

AND THAT'S WHY, DESPITE OUR ~~NAME-CALLING~~ DIFFERENCES AND ~~DEFAMATIONS OF EACH OTHERS'~~ ~~CHARACTER~~ ARGUMENTS AND ALL THE ~~HORRIBLE~~ *PASSIONATE* THINGS WE SAY TO EACH OTHER, THESE ALWAYS WILL BE MY FRIENDS.

ST. JOHN THE BAPTIST PARISH LIBRARY
2920 NEW HIGHWAY 51
LAPLACE, LOUISIANA 70068

(THOUGH ASK ME AGAIN AFTER
THE NEXT ELECTION SEASON STARTS.)

(I WONDER HOW DIFFICULT IT IS TO MOVE TO CANADA?)

ACKNOWLEDGMENTS

First things first: A special thank-you to the group of friends, sitting at a restaurant table next to mine as I waited for my own friends to show up, whose cordiality gave way to hostility in a fashion so rapid as to plant the idea for this book's title in my head. Years of witnessing arguments like this have gradually informed the creation of this book, but for whatever reason, this table of strangers going from Jekyll to Hyde and back is what provided the spark. Thanks, strangers, and sorry for occasionally staring.*

Of course, an idea is worthless without the means to execute on it. I worked on this book in secret—to the exasperation of many, I'm superstitious about sharing or even revealing unfinished work—but that doesn't mean I did any of this alone.

My parents supplied every tool imaginable to help me become proficient as a writer and illustrator (and computer programmer, baseball player, *Mike Tyson's Punch-Out!!* world champion, and more). But beyond tools, they instilled the importance of embracing creativity, pursuing curiosity, coloring way outside the lines (just not on the walls please), and rejecting the notion that hard work and self-discipline are antonymous with having fun. Graduating from the vague idea stage to the book you now hold in your hands required all of these tools and lessons. This story doesn't even exist, much less thrive, without their guidance.

Anyone who knows me well also knows the funding stage of this endeavor is my idea of a nightmare. So some special thanks are in order to a few people who made it less horrifying (and even, sometimes, pretty exhilarating).

- My girlfriend, Chrystal, not only promoted the book online way more than I ever had the nerve to, but she also politely but very-slightly-menacingly put the screws to her coworkers to order a copy (a point made more amusing by the fact that they're my coworkers too).
- Mindy (one of my best friends since we met way back in 1990) and her husband, Mark (same, albeit way back in 2013), did a similar number on our many mutual friends.

- My friend Ashley (the only person in Massachusetts who prefers her Sox be white instead of red) canvassed much of the East Coast while also snapping up the first and last backer copies at the beginning and end of the funding campaign.
- A number of other folks on the Inkshares label—most prominently Peter Ryan, Nicola Sarjeant, Craig and Margo Munro, and P. H. James—went to bat for me at every stage of this process. (Look them up if you're looking for something new to read.)

Lastly, whether you're reading a signed backer copy or you found this at your local bookstore many months later, thank YOU for reading (and hopefully enjoying) this book. It was and remains a treat to bring it to you. If you have any thoughts you wish to share, get in touch, because I always appreciate hearing them (even the bad ones).

*(*Thanks to the dogs in my life, past and present—Lucy, Crystal with no H, Molly, and Nina—who taught me that sometimes the best way to deal with an argument no one can win is to turn your head 45 degrees and look at everyone like they've lost their minds.)*

ABOUT THE AUTHOR

By day, Billy O'Keefe writes mostly unamusing web code. By moonlight, he is a writer and illustrator of delightful words and pictures. He enjoys both halves of his day. You can find samples of everything at his website, www.billyok.com. Billy lives in Printers Row, Chicago, and *These Are My Friends on Politics* is his first book.

LIST OF PATRONS

This book was made possible in part by the following grand patrons who preordered the book on inkshares.com. Thank you.

Alexander Barnes

Allyson Morch

Amy K. Nielsen

Angela Parker Kennedy

Ashley Brent

Brandon Hofer

Brent Seberhagen

Carlos Jackson

Chester "Fat Daddy" Greczkowski

Chris La Pelusa

Christina M. Raddi

Chrystal Marie, Hayden, and Addy

David Darling

Demitrius Berkley Thomas

Dennis Nolte

Diana K. Hayes

Erica M. Coriglione

Gina and Rob Carroll

Hector Moreno

Jennifer Chrzanowski

Joseph A. Monroe

Lee Ann Harper

Leigh C. Novak

Lisa A. Schryver

Luis Hernandez

Mark and Natalka Wegener

Mark Wegener and Melinda Cusentino

Mary Rivera

Michael Koretzky

Michael Link

Michael Vesper

Nate and Jackie Schultz

Nicole M. Denk

Olive Yew Jewels

P. H. James

Professor Bob O'Keefe and the DePaul University Department of Marketing

Rabeeah I. Patail

Ramond and Debbie Chiaramonte

Rebecca M. Whamond

Rob Neff

Robert, Barbara, and Nina O'Keefe

Sarah Beck

Scott Mathews

Scott R. Heimberg

Seth Runkle

Tabi Card

Tara Puckey

The Sun City Sunday

William Smitrovich

William, Vicky, and Audrey O'Keefe

INKSHARES

Inkshares is a crowdfunded book publisher. We democratize publishing by having readers select the books we publish—we edit, design, print, distribute, and market any book that meets a preorder threshold. Interested in making a book idea come to life? Visit inkshares.com to find new book projects or start your own.